STAFFORD CLIFF

1000

HOME IDEAS

PHOTOGRAPHS BY CHRISTIAN SARRAMON

Everybody thinks about their home. When you're young, if you have your own room, it becomes your world, and you soon set about personalising it, making it your private domain. When you leave home, you start to create another one – and you wonder how you're going to manage with all the decisions you'll need to make. Some folk dread it, and others just can't wait to go shopping. But not everything is available from a shop. You'll need ideas, too. What type of floor will you have: carpets, mats, rugs or floorboards? Stone or brick, maybe? You will inherit some of the elements, and certain decisions will be made for you – by the space or the previous owners. No matter, you'll want to tailor it to your needs. Maybe you can't change the floors, the walls, the ceilings or the staircase, but you'll almost certainly need to repaint or replace some things, move them about – doors, perhaps, or even windows; an extension, a home office, a bigger bathroom. Even if the task is too big for you to undertake yourself, don't be put off. If you know the effect you want, you can easily find a local builder or craftsman to do it for you. It's all a matter of choices, and there will be dozens of them; each one you make will say something about you, or your partner – or your parents. A terrifying prospect, and one you'll need to be prepared for – not only at the start of your homemaking life, but throughout it; when you move, or when you refurnish – as your circumstances, your influences, or your income changes. The questions go on and on – but so do the answers – over 1000 of them, all collected here in the work of the brilliant French photographer Christian Sarramon – who has spent 30 years photographing some of the most extraordinary, ideas-filled homes in the world.

OPENINGS

& CLOSINGS

When we're looking to move or buy a new property, we all know that the quirky little details in a house can be the difference between a 'yes' and a 'no'. An interesting window, pretty or unusual ceiling mouldings or nice-looking doors will make a place more individual and, therefore, more desirable – and, if you're ripping everything out to give yourself extra space, take care not to remove those features that attracted you in the first place. If your doors are not great, consider replacing them with folding, sliding or even framed glass doors. A modern front door on a traditional house can create a dynamic effect. Windows where you don't expect them are intriguing, as are unusually shaped frames or fittings. Round windows, for instance, always look special, as do those with coloured or patterned glass. If you don't have a feature window, don't let that stop you. With a bit of inspiration, you can add one where you would most like some extra light, and it's easy to pick up a reclaimed window frame. Failing that, think 'outside the box' about window treatments: slatted blinds, beaded curtains, pretty vintage lace or even wooden shutters will make a more individual alternative to off-the-peg curtains. Or consider using frosted glass – so that you can ensure your privacy without losing your precious light.

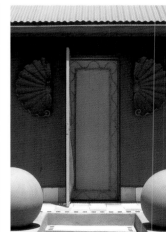

INTEREST

UNDER FOOT

I recall somebody saying to me years ago, when I moved into a new house, that 'it won't feel like a home until you've got the carpets down'. And in a sense it was true. The floor coverings softened the sound and somehow made everything feel finished, even with only one sofa and some cushions on the floor. Then, of course, there's the smell of new carpet – it's quite sensual, like the smell in a new car. But, over the past 20 years, wall-to-wall carpets have fallen out of fashion in modern interiors. Think of any of the trendy restaurants that you've been to recently, you very rarely see carpet these days. First, there was sisal: ethnic and satisfying, but difficult to clean and horrible on bare feet. And pattern was definitely out, as decorators and designers began using hard flooring: floorboards in rare woods, stone and marble. Now, a wide range of wood or wood-effect flooring is available to everyone, and people are even rescuing old floorboards from salvage yards and building sites. At the same time, stone, brick, tiles and even smooth pebbles began to be popular. These are ideal for bathrooms or areas with underfloor heating. Now, things are changing once again. Colour is back – on large 'designer' rugs with bold modern graphics, that are rather like putting a painting on the floor.

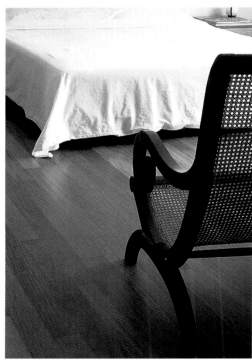

STEPS &

BANISTERS

The original features in a house are like its fingerprints. They are the authentic ingredients, added by the architect or the builder, to make it unique. They show the time in which it was built, its style and its creators' handwriting. If it's a period house, then those features will probably be from an amazing catalogue of builders' suppliers. But there was a time – during the 1970s – when people wanted their homes to look 'modern' and DIY enthusiasts began ripping out mouldings, skirtings and fireplaces and covering panelled doors and stair banisters with plywood. Now the tide has turned: people want a little bit of tradition, and reclamation yards are doing big business in authentic period features. Most defining of all the elements is the staircase, which can offer a spectacular flourish at the heart of the house – often in prime position when you open the front door. Some of the most impressive modern interiors often feature an open staircase in metal or glass, or a sculptural curving creation down which to glide. Not everyone wants to replace their staircase, but if you are adding an extra floor or converting the attic, you may need to add one. In which case, from spiral to dog leg to fire escape to ladder; from metal to wood to stone to concrete, there is a world of possibilities.

COOKING

& EATING

Our homes respond to the way we live: the stages of our life, our income and our domestic set up – single, married or a family unit. In the 1950s, the 'work triangle' concept was formulated, establishing the ideal position for the cooker, the fridge and the sink unit, so that a housewife didn't have to walk too far – if at all. Rapid changes in attitudes towards cooking, eating and entertaining, and massive advances in technology have had a bigger impact on the kitchen than anywhere else in the home. In the 1920s, the suburban kitchen was a tiny, rarely seen work station at the back of the building, but in the 1990s it was enlarged and moved to a prime position with high-tech equipment and state-of-the-art joinery. Now, with the move towards city centre living and with the abundance of tempting neighbourhood restaurants, some young people choose not to cook at all. Along the way, we had the smart modern kitchen and formal dining room, the family room with its cooking, eating, entertaining and general family life free-for-all, and the restaurant-style kitchen with its industrial-looking cookers, steamers, coffee makers and even glass-fronted fridges. None of these solutions have become inappropriate, it's up to you, your style and how you want to live.

SHELF

LIFE

When I've asked people what they look for when entering someone's house, the most popular answer has been: 'Their books. If I see what they read, I know their interests and what type of person they are'. Sounds obvious, but in most cases it's subconscious. We respond to things that are similar to our own, and books – or the lack of them – sometimes say more about us than we might like. Photography books, history books, art books, children's books, paperbacks or first editions tell a host of stories, and if the room has a large bookshelf, or even wall-to-wall, floor-to-ceiling shelving, our eyes dance across it, enjoying the rhythm, the colour and the intrigue. But don't overdo it; you're not living in a library. Allow space on the shelves for a few objects – pictures, perhaps, or beautiful boxes – things that make a visual break. Even if you don't have lots of books, there are plenty of other things that will shine on a shelf, and if you don't normally collect things, then having a generous set of shelves will soon inspire you to fill it. Best of all, add some concealed lighting here and there, to give a bit of sparkle at night. Finally, decide how you will group your books – by subject, by size, by ownership, by frequency of use or – and this, too, reveals something about the homeowner – by the colour of the spine.

COVETED

CUPBOARDS

Some say that a house can never have enough cupboards, and minimalists know that the look they love – bare surfaces and cool empty spaces – can only be achieved by monastic discipline and floor-to-ceiling storage behind seamless white doors. But it's also a fact that the more storage space you have, the more you hoard and the less you chuck out. I once interviewed someone who told me: 'We only allow one more thing into the house if we take something out'. It's a good intention, but one that few of us can maintain. The rest of us need plenty of space to store things away, but at the same time, to know exactly where to find everything. To that end, having a large beautiful cupboard is a two-fold joy. As opposed to built-in storage, it has the benefit of being able to be moved about. Choose a simple country style or an embellished ethnic piece, or you might prefer something from a particular design period like the 1920s or '30s. The sort of thing that gets abandoned during house clearances can often be surprisingly inexpensive. And once you've got it through the front door and – heaven forbid – up the stairs, don't stop short of customising it. Strip off the varnish, apply paint effects or cover it with bold wallpaper, and, most importantly – fit in lots of extra shelves.

QUIET

CORNERS

Whether your house is large or small, whether you live alone or with a big family, setting aside a small corner of one room – preferably near a window – for a desk, a comfortable chair and an efficient lamp, can create one of the most beguiling and special places in your home. Everyone will have a preference over its position – a spot where you get the morning sun, a nice view or simply a bit of peace and quiet. Even if you work all day in an office, a place at home where you can leave your letters, your books, your laptop or your hobbies out on a table, will be very appealing. I don't mean an enormous desk covered with papers, telephones and all the inherent pressure that spells hard work. There are all sorts of interesting tables you could use, large or small, as well as consoles, writing bureauxs and roll-tops. And if there are a few shelves, a cupboard, storage drawers and fresh flowers – even better. Keep it domestic, unless, of course, you work from home. If that's the case, you may need a devoted room – keep it away from the temptations of family and pets, TV or cooking. Should you run out of space or your work starts to take over your home-life, you can always follow the lead of such writers as Dylan Thomas and Charles Dickens who found peace and quiet in a shed at the end of the garden.

WALLS OF

WONDER

Rooms tell many stories – as you'll know if you've ever visited the museum homes of painters, writers, collectors or famous explorers. Though no longer stuffed with the clutter of everyday life, these houses are filled with memories. If it's a house full of character, that identity will come from the person's possessions, what they collected and how it is displayed on shelves, in cabinets, on tables – or most importantly on the walls. Designers and artists love to surround themselves with pictures, paintings, prints and framed momentoes of all kinds. Explorers bring back maps, posters, bus tickets and things that remind them of their journeys. People with children will put up school drawings. But for some, having the confidence to hang things, personal things, quirky things on the walls, takes a certain bravery that they may not have. Where's the best position? What's the most suitable frame? Perhaps the solution is to concentrate first on one small space – maybe in the hall or a bedroom. Approach the wall as a page on a scrapbook rather than a gallery wall, and don't think that you have to use expensive images or one-off artworks. Displaying the most unusual and personal things often proves to be the most interesting, generating the most compliments and engaging your eye for the longest time.

LIGHT

MY FIRE

What style of fireplace goes with what style of room? Should you match it to the architecture or your home furnishings? Do you want a fireplace with a big mantelpiece or a small one? Do you need a mantelpiece at all? Perhaps a simple cut-out surround would suffice – maybe a square or framed circle. You might think that it depends on whether you want to have 'real' flames, but now – with many types of 'designer' fires available, there are almost no rules. The deciding factor might be heat. If you want your fire to heat the room, there are specific products to suit your needs. But there are also requirements to consider concerning flues, chimneys, size of opening, safety and so forth. On the other hand, if it's just the decorative elements that you're after, a flickering flame to look at and a shelf on which to display your trophies – then there are no limits. This might make it easier to decide, or harder. Visit suppliers' showrooms and see what's on offer – and be prepared for a surprise: flames flickering from a row of white pebbles, ceramic pinecones or a jumble of letters of the alphabet; fireplaces that look more like framed artworks or something from a Swiss ski lodge. You can even have a smokeless fire in a glass cylinder in the centre of a coffee table.

COLOUR &

TEXTURE

'Calm down and don't get so emotional.' I bet somebody has said that to you before – but have they said it about your living room? Of all the things that you can do to a room, adding colour is considered the most personal, the most emotional. Colour is fundamental to our wellbeing. Many studies have been done into the psychology of colour and its effects on our mood – think of those used in street signs, on traffic lights and safety notices. From an early age, we respond to certain colours – red for danger; black for mourning (or in some cultures, white). In the home, we know that a white room reflects the light; that blue and green are a good fresh palette for bathrooms; that red is cosy and welcoming. It sounds simple, but it's not. Add to this, the element of texture: gloss or matt, embossed or even perforated. Property developers all agree that if you want to appeal to the greatest number of people, and get a quick sale, then you should keep it neutral. Aside from that, why would you? Colour is so easy to apply – you can change a room between breakfast and lunch. Start with a small area – a door, maybe, or a window frame or a single wall. Trust your instincts – your emotions. Colour is the clash of cymbals at the end of a Mahler concert. How could you go home without it?

REACHING

OUTWARDS

Trends in fashion have a huge influence over what we buy and wear, but trends in home furnishing change more slowly, and are affected not only by the availability of exciting new products and technology – things like digital TV and LED lighting – but by the changes in our domestic habits, and by what we see elsewhere in the world. The most radical development for many years, stimulated by cheaper air fares and our holiday trips to hotter, more exotic destinations, has been our desire for a more open-air lifestyle at home. New hotels all around the world now offer alfresco beds looking onto elephant watering holes; bathtubs, showers and infinity pools amongst tropical vegetation; and, most seductive of all, cooking and eating outdoors. Even in the coolest countries, cafés and restaurants with outdoor seating are now commonplace. At last, the back doors at home have been flung open and the wobbly metal table and folding plastic chairs can be replaced by more sophisticated cooking equipment on decking that supports a generous dining table, chairs and even stylish all-weather wicker sofas, seats and coffee tables, enhanced by solar lighting, patio heating and a ceramic chiminea. Given current predictions for climate change, canopy beds cannot be far behind.

Acknowledgements

So now you know. No home is ordinary or dull, and nor does it need to be. It's just a matter of opening your eyes and seeing the possibilities. Whether it's a new window, a glass door, an old cupboard or a brightly coloured rug, ideas are everywhere and every homeowner needs as many as they can get. Inspiration can come from visiting a store, a hotel or a country house. But often it's from something in a book, a magazine, or on TV. Sometimes it can be found by simply visiting a neighbour. **Stafford Cliff, London**

The homes on these pages are the loving creations of many people around the world, and I would like to thank all those who, over the last twenty years, have opened their doors and welcomed me into their home so that I could see their treasures. I would also like to express my warmest appreciation to all the architects, designers, decorators, stylists, journalists and assistants who were essential on the photographic shoots. With many special thanks to Stafford Cliff, who has produced a brilliant design from my modest photographs. And also to Jane O'Shea for her enthusiasm and kindness. And, of course, thanks to my wife, Inès, and my two sons, Diego and Kim, for their help and endless patience every day. Christian Sarramon, Paris

Page 16 top and bottom row, centre: Sunfold Systems make high-quality, high-security and highly insulating, sound-deadening aluminium panelled front doors. Design details are highlighted through the use of triple-glazed glass and stainless steel inlays. Their flush surfaces and clear aesthetic lines represent straightforward elegance in its purest form.
Tel: +44 (0) 1953 423423; www.sunfold.com.

Page 17 (except for bottom right): Urban Front are specialist designers and manufacturers of unique, elegant and contemporary doors, made from hardwood and stainless steel. Each door has a reinforced steel core.
Tel: +44 (0) 1494 778787; www.urbanfront.co.uk.

Page 154 fireplaces: top left, from Planika. A series of products that create real fire without any smoke. Incorporates an automatic, electronically controlled ethanol fuel feeding system.
Tel: +48 52 364 11 63; www.planikafires.com.
Top right, from Smart Fire Ltd. The EcoSmart fire is an Australian innovation – an environmentally friendly open fireplace. Flueless, it does not require any installation or utility connection for fuel supply. Fuelled by methylated spirits, it burns cleanly and is virtually maintenance free.
Tel: +44 (0) 20 7173 5014; www.ecosmartfire.com.

Editorial Director Jane O'Shea
Designer Stafford Cliff
Photographer Christian Sarramon
Design Assistant Katherine Case
Editor Laura Herring
Production Vincent Smith,
Marina Asenjo

First published in 2008 by
Quadrille Publishing Limited
Alhambra House
27–31 Charing Cross Road
London
WC2H 0LS
www.quadrille.co.uk

Design and layout © 2008
Quadrille Publishing Limited
Text © 2008 Stafford Cliff

Cataloguing in Publication Data:
a catalogue record for this book is available from the British Library.

ISBN: 978 184400 617 5

Printed in China